Life Skills

Learning

with

RAINBOW KIDS

Volume 1

Stories, Articles, Activities, Quizzes and More
to Spark Imagination and Joy

First Edition 2023

ISBN 978-81-966182-9-2 (Paperback)
ISBN 978-81-966182-1-6 (Ebook)

Published by: **Rainbow Village Private Limited**
www.rainbow-kids.app
Email: info@rainbow-kids.app

Hello Kids,

We are very excited to bring to you the first edition of the Rainbow Kids book series!

We hope you enjoy this issue as much as we do, and find it interesting to learn about new things or remember a few things you already know!

We have a few exciting stories to share, which include Pip who comes to adore his unique laugh, the two brothers, Jay and Sid realizing how being truthful makes things easier, the two friends Maya and Roy playfully learning a new skill without giving up and a few more.

When days are not going as expected, we can be thankful for the things we already have (check out "I Am Thankful For...") or understand and manage our not-so-pleasant emotions using a few tips (check out "What Am I Feeling?"), to make ourselves feel better again!

Don't forget to try out the board game that you can make and play with your family and friends.

Wishing you a lot of fun and happy reading!
The Rainbow Kids Team

Includes

The Goose Boy

Pip was a little boy who was very ticklish. From his head to his toes, Pip's skin couldn't be touched even with the lightest brush, for it sent him into peals of laughter.

That wasn't all. Whenever Pip laughed, he sounded like a honking goose!

"Hoonk! Hooonk! Hoonk!" Pip laughed and laughed when his hair was brushed, when he took a bath, even when the wind brushed his cheeks!

Pip's first day of school arrived, and he thought, "it will all be alright; there will be other kids who will laugh as much as me."

However, when Pip got to his class, it wasn't long before the pages of a book made him laugh.

"Hoonk! Hoonk! Hooonk!" Pip laughed, and his cheeks turned tomato red when everyone else began to stare.

One little boy started to laugh too. The sound of the boy's laughter made Pip laugh even harder. On and on, he went on until more children joined in.

As Pip laughed, he noticed something; his laughter was the only one that sounded so loud! The other children's laughter sounded so different!

Embarrassed, Pip promised himself, "I will not laugh again." But this wasn't easy, for Pip's ticklishness made him roll around with laughter all the time. It wasn't long before every child in the school knew Pip as the Goose Boy.

"I'm never going to laugh," Pip told himself once again when the school day ended. "I don't like my laugh. I wish I was like the other kids and not so odd!"

Just then, Pip's next door neighbour, dressed as a clown for a performance who was passing by, overheard him and asked, "Oh Pip, what's so bad about your laughing?"

"My laugh is ugly; that's what's so bad," Pip said,
stomping his foot on the ground. "Whenever I laugh,
I sound like a goose, and everyone laughs
at me."

The clown nodded in understanding and said, "I have a few visits to make around the city this evening. Join me if you are interested, after checking with your parents, I would like to show you something."

With his mum's permission, Pip followed the clown throughout the city on his scheduled visits. They visited a birthday party, a community centre and a children's hospital.

Some of the children they visited were either feeling down or struggling with pain. But when the clown walked through the doors and said, "Hello, kids! Who's ready to laugh?", the children's frowns turned into bright smiles as they watched the clown do his silly walks, sing his funny songs, juggle balls, hunk his large red nose and throw pies in the air.

They laughed, laughed and laughed, and for that time, their troubles melted away, and they were as happy as could be.

Pip, who laughed from almost anything, couldn't help to laugh along.

"Hooonk! Hooonk-hoonk-hooooonk!" Pip laughed and laughed.

When the children heard his hearty goose-like laughter, it made them even happier. Soon Pip and children were all in stitches, rolling on the floor with laughter.

"Do you see now, Pip?" the clown asked when they left the hospital.

Pip frowned as he looked up at the sky. The sun was already setting, and purple, gold, and orange clouds drifted lazily across the sky.

"I think I do," Pip said, still thoughtful. He thought of how the clown spent his day bringing joy to those children who needed it the most.

It didn't matter that he was old, didn't perform in a circus, or had the newest, brightest clown outfits. The clown loved his job, and that was enough for him. Nothing else mattered, not his age, not his looks, or how he went from place to place.

The clown looked at him, eager to hear what Pip had learned.

Pip looked at the clown with sparkling eyes and said, "I shouldn't worry about being different, or how my laugh sounds, for it is that what makes me special."

The clown nodded and, seeing Pip had much more to say, murmured, "go on."

"Everyone is different. We all look different, laughter comes in many ways, and so do skin colours and languages. But that shouldn't keep us from being the best person we can be and loving ourselves for who we are. Only when we truly love ourselves and embrace our differences can we truly do something special."

The clown smiled, proud of Pip's quick thinking.

Suddenly, Pip stopped in the middle of the sidewalk and declared, "I may sound like a goose when I laugh, but it sounds so jolly and I love it. It brings happiness and laughter to others too! I'm going to use my laugh from now on to spread joy to everyone I see!"

The clown smiled, squeezed his red nose, and then hugged Pip tightly. This made Pip laugh again and the two laughed together all their way back home.

The next day at school, Pip shared his laughter with everyone. He didn't even have to get tickled; whenever he saw a child frown, Pip gifted them with a laugh that turned their frown into bright smiles and peals of laughter.

Eventually, everyone who had made fun of Pip and called him names looked up to Pip and his courage to embrace who he was, love himself and share his laughter with the world.

"Pip, your laughter is like sunshine on a rainy day," his teacher said one day. "Never stop being who you are and sharing your laughter with the world!"

Why Do We Recycle?

Did you know that we all have a big role
to play in saving our planet?

That's right — each one of us can take small steps
every day to create a big change!

And this change begins with something known as
recycling.

Let's understand what recycling means and how we can help our planet with a little bit of knowledge and practice.

Everything we throw "away" as waste goes somewhere. Have you ever wondered where would all this rubbish end up?

The truck that comes regularly to take the rubbish dumps it in a place called a *landfill*.

Think of it as a sort of dumping site where piles and piles of waste get thrown into a pit in the ground every day.

What is recycling? 

Before tossing all our rubbish into the bin, we can sort out the "recyclables" and put them instead in the recycling bins outside our homes and schools.

Recycling

These bins are emptied into trucks, which take all our recyclables to the recycling center to be further sorted, cleaned and organised. They are then piled and pressed together into neat little boxes, ready to be used for making new items.

What can we recycle?

Before throwing all our waste as rubbish, we can sort and separate the recyclable materials and put them in the separate recycling bins.

Glass

- Glass bottles
- Glass jars

Plastic

- Water bottles
- Soft drink/Juice bottles
- Shampoo bottles
- Ceaning product bottles
- Milk bottles

Aluminium

- Drink cans
- Food tins
- Aluminium foil (without food residue)
- Aluminium lids/caps

Paper

- Magazines
- Books
- Papers/Newspapers
- Cardboard boxes
- Egg cartons

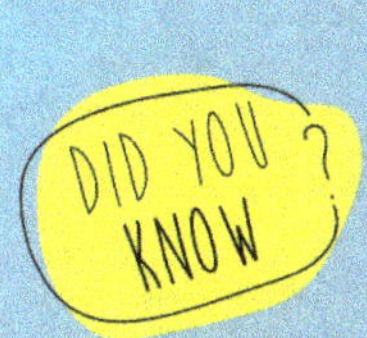

This symbol is the commonly used recycling symbol, which shows that the item can be recycled.

Why do we have to recycle?

Recycling helps the environment in many ways:

Reduces landfill that pollutes air, water and soil, by recycling our waste.

Conserves natural resources such as wood, water and minerals by reducing the need to get raw materials to make new things.

Reduces air and water pollution by reducing the need for raw materials.

Saves a lot of energy, as making the products from recycled materials consumes less energy than making them from raw materials.

Recycling is easy and free and all of us can take part in it as much as possible.

Besides recycling, we can also help the environment by:

REDUCE

Reducing the waste we create by using less plastic and paper when possible.

Reusing items whenever we can or passing them over to others who could use them, instead of throwing them away as rubbish.

REUSE

These simple steps go a long way in protecting the environment that nurtures us.

So are YOU ready to save the Earth and be a planet doctor?

Why wouldn't the shrimp share his treasure?

Because he was a little shellfish!

What kind of tree can fit in one hand?

A palm tree!

What has a ton of ears but can't hear a thing?

A corn field!

How do you get a mouse to smile?

Say cheese!

What is at the end of everything?

The letter "g".

What animal is best at hitting a ball?

A bat!

Why was the maths book sad?

Because it had lots of problems!

What has two legs and cannot walk?

A pair of trousers!

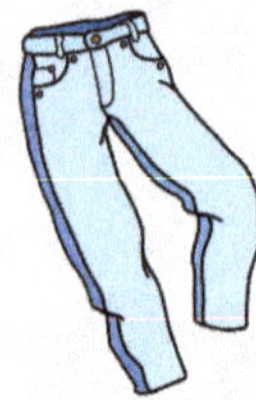

Why did the girl toss the butter out the window?

So she could see a butter-fly!

Why do birds fly south in the winter?

It is faster than walking!

Making My Own Board Game

Ever tried to make your own board game?
Have fun making and playing one of the
classic board games, the "Mill".

The mill is a two-player game and takes around 10 minutes to make the mill board and 10 to 15 minutes to play the game.

What is the goal of the game?

Capture seven of your opponent's pieces by forming "mills" or create a trap so that it is impossible for the opponent to move.

A mill is formed when a player places three of their pieces (of the same colour) on adjacent circles in a line.

What's required?

- The mill board.
- 18 pieces of two different colours (nine pieces of each colour). You can use rocks, buttons or pieces from other board games.

How to make the mill board?

1. Take a plain paper (A4 size) or cardboard.

2. Using a bright-coloured pen or marker and a ruler, draw three squares of varying sizes, one inside the other, with the smallest square towards the centre.

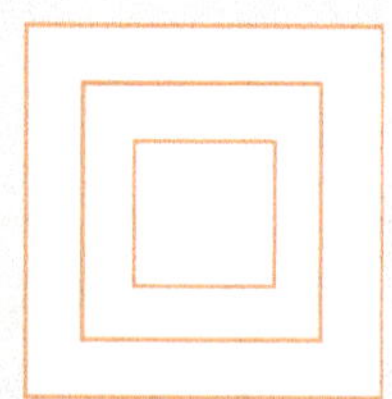

3. Draw a circle on each of the four corners and the centre of each of the lines on all the three squares. There are eight circles on each square.

4. Draw lines connecting the circles at the centre of the lines, on each side of the squares.

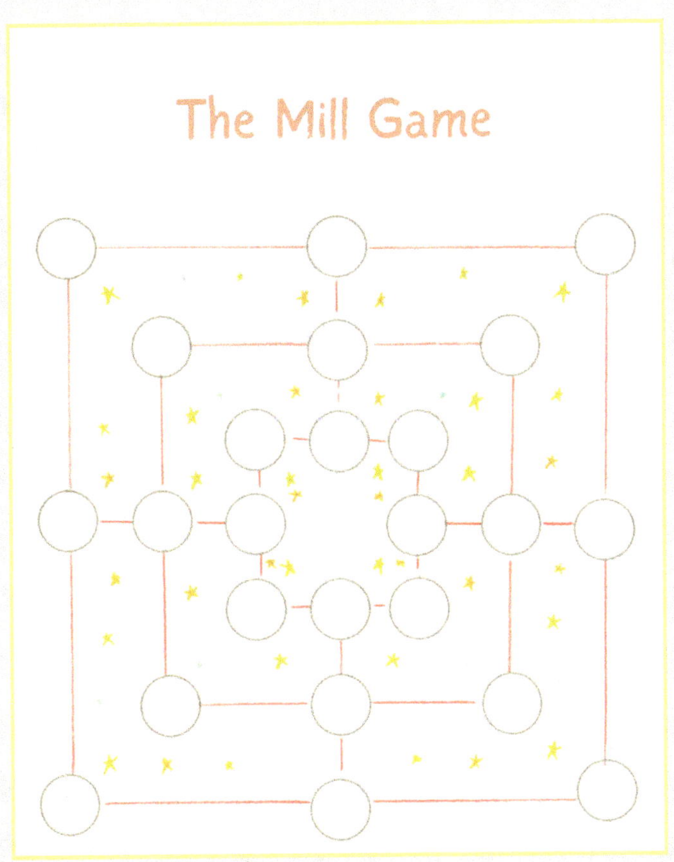

The Mill Game

How to play?

1. Toss a coin to decide who goes first.

2. The players take turns to place each of their nine pieces on vacant circles on the board. If a player forms a mill, they must remove an opponent's piece, that is not part of a mill from the board.

3. Once all the nine pieces have been placed, the players move one of their existing pieces to an adjacent free circle along a line during their turn. If a player forms a mill, they must remove an opponent's piece, that is not part of a mill from the board.

4. When a player has only three pieces left, the player can jump their piece to any vacant circle on the board instead of just the adjacent circle.

5. The game ends when a player has only two pieces left or is unable to move. The game ends in a draw when both players agree to draw or the same move occurs three times in a row.

The Flower of Joy

The little boy, Jay had a big, kind heart. He made everyone who crossed his path smile. But there was one little girl at his school who never smiled.

She always wore a frown and looked at the ground. Jay told her jokes, invited her to play, did silly things and even sat next to her, but not even his friendship gestures made her happy.

"I don't get it; why can't I make her smile?" Jay told his brother Sid.

Sid frowned thoughtfully. Then his eyes brightened up, "have you tried giving her a flower?"

Jay looked at his brother, puzzled. "A flower, why?"

"Mom always smiles when Daddy gives her flowers, even when she's had a pretty bad day", Sid said.

Jay smiled and nodded, "you are right, I'll give her a flower!"

The next day, before he went to school, he took a flower from his mother's vase. She always had the prettiest, red, orange, pink, purple and even blue flowers!

When Jay saw the little girl enter the classroom, he ran up to her and gave her the rose.

The little girl looked up at him and smiled shyly. Jay had done it; he made the girl smile!

The very next day, before he went to school, he took another flower from the vase and gave it to the girl, who smiled again!

Jay was so happy that he kept on bringing her flowers every morning.

But one day, Mom noticed her flowers were disappearing.

"Where are my flowers going?" Mom asked out loud one morning as she looked at her vase, which only had two flowers left in it!

Jay's stomach did a flip. He wondered if he would be in trouble and got very scared. He was about to say something, but his brother shook his head. "Go on to school; I will talk to her."

Glad that his brother would talk to Mom, Jay went to school without saying anything.

That afternoon, Mom greeted them with a chocolate cake.

"What's this for?" Jay asked, puzzled.

Mom smiled, "just a little something to celebrate your brother's honesty and kindness."

Jay looked at Sid, puzzled. Sid beamed and shrugged.

What is going on? Jay thought.

The next morning, while Sid was playing with friends, Jay asked Mom, "what makes Sid such an honest and kind son?"

Mom hugged Jay and said, "Every morning, he takes a flower from our vase and gives it to a girl at school to make her smile. Isn't that the kindest thing you've ever heard?"

Jay gasped, and his eyes widened, "the one who took the flowers wasn't Sid; it was me!"

Mom looked at him with big eyes, "why didn't you say anything?"

Jay lowered his head, "I thought you would be mad at me for taking the flowers without asking. Sid said he would talk to you, I thought he would tell you it had been me, but he lied."

Mom hugged Jay tightly, "oh, Jay, being honest is very important. Even by omission, lies are still lies, and nothing good comes from them."

Jay thought about his mother's words and how he felt when Sid got all the credit for being so kind and honest. It did not feel good, and he should have told Mom the truth right away, not let his brother speak for him.

Looking at Mom with sparkling eyes, Jay said, "from now on, I'll speak for myself and tell the truth, no matter what."

Mom smiled proudly at her son.

The next day, she greeted him with a bouquet of flowers from her garden, "here, take these to your friend."

Jay thanked Mom and rushed to school to give his new friend the flowers.

When the girl saw the beautiful flowers, she beamed with joy. Her smile was the brightest he had ever seen.

"Are all these for me?" She asked shyly.

Jay nodded eagerly.

The girl kept on smiling, "these are too many for me. I only need one."

Jay watched as the girl handed each child in the classroom a flower and kept the last for herself.

"I love flowers," the girl told him.

"Every morning, before school, I would walk through the fields of flowers in my hometown. But since I moved to this larger town, all I see are flowers in vases or flower shops.

It made me so sad. I miss my town, home and most of all, my grandma. Then, you began to give me flowers every morning and it made me so happy! I no longer missed home and grandma as much, and I even started making friends, all because of your kindness."

Jay's heart was full of joy, for the girl had been honest with him and told him the reason for her sadness. It felt good to be honest, and make someone smile!

From that day on, the girl and Jay became best friends.

What happened with Sid, you may ask? He too learned, that honesty was better than telling lies.

Riddles

It belongs to you. But your friends use it more. What is it?

1

What has a face and hands, but can't hold anything or smile?

2

What gets wet while drying?

3

What is so fragile that saying its name breaks it?

4

"I have no life, but I can die. What am I?"

5

If there are three cookies and you take away two, how many do you have?

6

"I am an odd number. Take away a letter and I become even. What number am I?"

7

What month has 28 days?

8

People buy me to eat, but never eat me. What am I?

9

The more there is the less you see.

10

What Am I Feeling?

We know when we are happy, and we all love that feeling. Sometimes we also feel sad. A few things scare us a lot, while many things excite us. Sometimes, we also get angry at someone or something.

These different feelings are called *emotions*.

Emotions help us understand and express what we feel.

Let us look at how a day went for Pia and how she felt during different situations. We can probably understand and relate to all of Pia's emotions.

Excitement

Today is Pia's birthday. Pia is feeling very excited as she opens her eyes in the morning. As soon as she gets out of her bed, she shouts "hooray", jumping up happily, with her arms raised high! It is her special day, and she wants to enjoy the day as best as she can!

We all feel excited for different reasons, for situations we love and anticipate so much, like getting what we wished for as a present, a visit from a favourite relative, or attending a party.

We show a lot of enthusiasm. Our heart beats faster and our stomach can flutter. Excitement is fun to express and share it with others.

Anger

Pia is painting a beautiful flower on an easel. Pia's sister, while walking past her, accidentally bumps into Pia without looking and spills paint from the tray onto the board. Pia is now bursting with anger and screams at her sister as her beautiful painting is ruined.

When someone says or does something we don't like, we get angry. We feel uncomfortable in the chest or the head.

We often express our anger by yelling, saying mean things or stomping our feet. Sometimes we continue to stay angry for a long time.

It is okay to feel angry when something upsets us. But it is not okay to hurt ourselves or others.

It is possible to take control of our anger by following a few easy tips. This will calm us faster and stop ruining our mood and our day.

What can I do when I feel angry?

I can breathe deeply a few times to calm myself, by breathing in slowly through the nose and breathing out through the mouth.

I can cry if I feel like crying or take some rest to make myself feel better.

I can do something I really like, such as playing with my favourite toy or listening to my favourite song.

I can walk away from the person or the situation that made me angry.

I can talk to someone I trust about what made me angry.

Fear

Pia is playing a game of hide-and-seek with her sister. Pia looked for her everywhere in the house, except in one place. It is an attic that is dark and damp with insects and spiders. Pia slowly climbs up the steps to the attic and suddenly screams and trembles with fear when she sees a huge spider hanging in front of her face.

We all have some kind of fear towards different things. Some fear darkness, while some others fear insects. Some fear spooky movies, while some others fear loud sounds. Some fear anything new, like new situations, new people or trying out new things.

Fear is a normal reaction in our body and mind to uncomfortable or scary things. When we are scared, our heart beats faster. We can sweat, shake, or cry. We may feel like hiding or running away.

When faced with fear, we can follow a few tips to calm us down and respond better.

What can I do when I feel scared?

I can take a few deep breaths and try again, even though I am scared. I may find out that it is not that scary at all!

I can talk to someone about what scares me.

Happiness

Pia answers the doorbell that rang and sees her grandpa at the door, holding a kitten with a bow.

We feel happy about little things and big things like eating our favourite food or enjoying our time with our family and friends. We express our happiness with a big smile and twinkling eyes and show a lot of energy to bounce around.

I am feeling...

Many of the emotions we feel like joy or excitement are pleasant to experience. We can also choose to get happy or excited for the routine things like waking up for a new day, eating hot and delicious meals or helping someone with their chores.

It helps our body and mind to function better when we continue to encourage these positive emotions. And it is always fun to be happy!

When we come across emotions that make us uncomfortable, we need not feel helpless. All of us, including grownups, experience such emotions. It is completely okay to feel what we feel, and it is not wrong.

We can learn to respond better to unpleasant emotions. Next time when we feel scared or angry like Pia, we can follow a few easy tips to make ourselves feel better. We are back to having a good time again!

The Three Questions

A retelling of a story by Leo Tolstoy

Once, there lived a king who had everything he wished for. One day, while holding court, he came across three questions.

If I had the answer to these questions, the king thought, I would never fail in anything.

The king asked himself, "what is the most important time for every action? Who is the most important person? What is the most important thing to do?"

These questions went over and over in the king's mind, day and night, so much so that the king could hardly sleep.

One day, the king announced throughout his kingdom a great reward for anyone who could answer his questions.

The learned men came to the king, but they all answered differently.

One man said, "It is impossible to decide the important time; your warriors are the important people, and expanding your kingdom is the important thing."

Another man said, "Good planning helps to determine the most important time; your councilors are the important people, and expanding knowledge is the important thing."

The third man said, "The wise men can help decide the important time; your priests are the important people, and the religious worship is the important thing to do."

The king was not happy with any of these answers. He then decided to consult a hermit, who was known for his wisdom.

The hermit lived in a remote forest and spoke to very few people. The next day the king, dressed in simple clothes, went with his soldiers to meet the hermit.

The king ordered his soldiers to stay behind and walked alone to the hermit.

The king said, "good day, wise hermit, I have come to you seeking answers to my three questions." Without waiting for an answer, he asked his questions.

The hermit, who looked old and weak, was busy digging the ground in front of his hut. He smiled at the king, said nothing, and continued digging.

"You look tired," said the king. "Let me help you."

As the sun began going down and it was getting dark, the king started to feel anxious to know the answers and stopped digging.

The king said, "hermit, I came to you to seek your answers. If you have none, say so, and I will return home."

Just then, a wounded man came running towards the hut and fainted on the ground, moaning with pain. The king carried the man into the hut and took care of his wound, and let him rest.

The next morning, the man said to the king, "Yesterday, I came here to harm you, for I was one of your enemies and was wounded on the way by your soldiers. But you saved my life. I would be delighted to serve you for the rest of my life."

The king listened to the man's tale, and his amusement grew the more he heard. He'd never considered that his actions could impact a person's life, which made him ponder his questions even more.

The king went looking for the hermit to ask his questions for the last time before returning to his palace.

The hermit, who was sowing seeds, looked at the king calmly and said, "Your questions have already been answered."

The king asked, "I do not understand, how?"

The hermit smiled, "Don't you see?"

The king frowned and thought about the hermit's words.

Suddenly, his eyes widened and twinkled in understanding, for the answers he had been seeking all these days came to him.

"I understand now!" The king exclaimed. "The important time, the important person, and the important thing to do applies to everyone, not just me."

The king recalled that the important time had been helping the hermit and tending to the injured man's wounds.

"My actions at that time made it the most important time to act, the present," murmured the king.

He concluded in that manner that the hermit and the wounded man were the important people.

"The persons whom we are with at the present are the important people," the king said, nodding, pleased with his deductions.

Helping the hermit and the wounded man had been the important thing to do, which in turn allowed the king to find his answers and saved his life, the king recalled, beaming with joy.

"Doing well to others in turn will bring good to us," the king announced.

The hermit seeing that the king understood perfectly, said, "king, now you can go and rule your kingdom wisely."

The king bowed in thanks and departed; for now, he had a greater understanding of how to be a great and just ruler to his people.

Cool Facts About Bees

Apart from the delicious honey, do you know what else buzzing bees are known for?

Bees are super important pollinators, helping plants grow and produce flowers, fruits and vegetables.

Though there are over 20,000 different types of bees, only one type of bees make honey, that we benefit from : the honeybees.

Bees perform the "waggle" dance to inform other bees about the food source they found: the flower nectar and pollen.

20th May is World Bee Day! World Bee Day celebrates the hard working bees, who play an important role in pollinating plants, that benefit plants, people, and the environment.

We turn on the tap and there it is — Water!

Could you ever imagine a day without water?

We need water to drink, to cook, and to keep ourselves and our environment clean. We need water for our plants and animals to survive, and to grow our food. Water is even required in factories to produce the things we use every day.

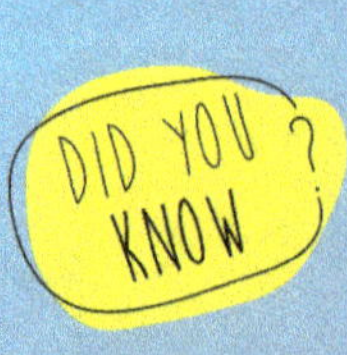

The amount of water used per person per day varies greatly depending on the availability. A minimum of about 100 litres per person per day is required for maintaining a healthy living.

Where does water come from?

We see water in so many places around us...

Let us see how it works.

The water cycle

The warmth from the sun heats water from different sources like oceans, rivers, and lakes, transforming the water into water vapour. This is called *evaporation*.

The water vapour is a tiny bit of water in the air all around us which we cannot see.

The vapour rises up in the air, cools, and forms clouds. This is called *condensation*.

When the clouds become heavy, the cooled vapour drops fall as precipitation or rain. The rainwater flows down to rivers, lakes, ponds or streams, gets collected in reservoirs, and also soaks into the ground.

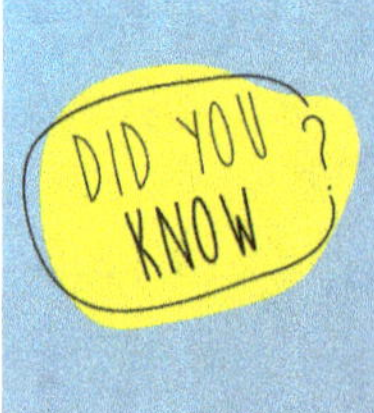

Though water makes up 70% of our earth, most of this water is salty and cannot be used. Only around 1% of water is freshwater and usable.

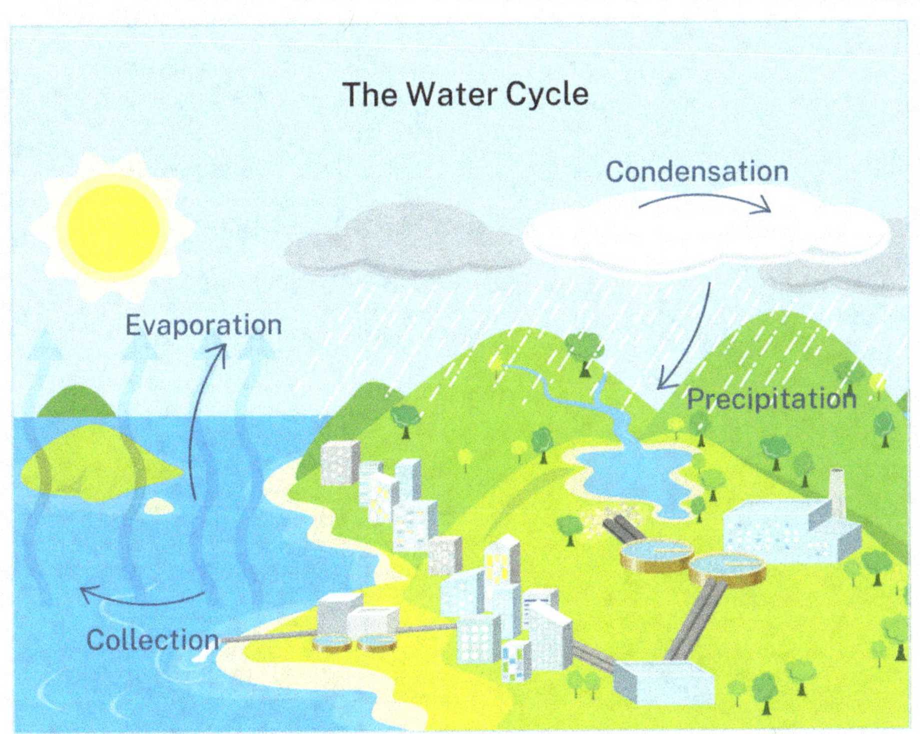

How do we get clean water?

Water that exists under the ground is called *groundwater*. Water from rivers, lakes or reservoirs is called *surface water*.

The source of water can be different depending on the place you are in, and the availability of water.

The water supply system

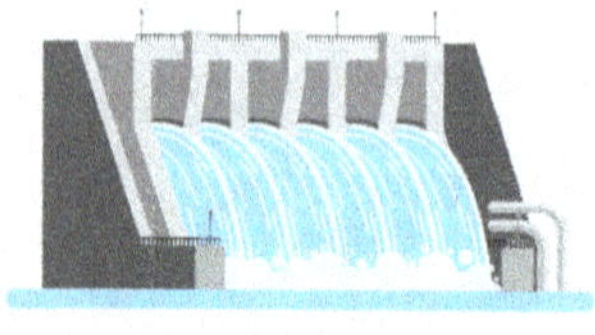

Water source

1 Using suitable tools, water is pulled from a source and is sent to a water treatment plant using underground pipes.

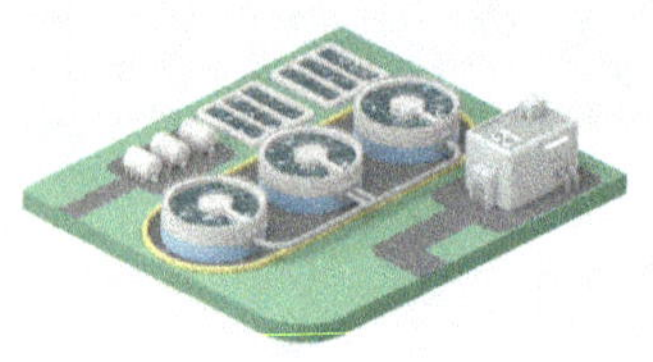
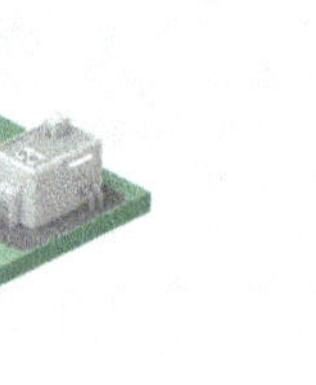

Water treatment plant

2 Water is filtered in the water treatment plant to remove unwanted particles. Disinfectants are added to remove harmful germs so water is safe to drink.

Water storage tank

3 The purified water is then sent to different water storage tanks.

Water distribution

4 Water from the storage tanks is distributed to nearby buildings, including schools, and houses, through connected pipes

Clean water is now available from our taps. We turn the tap on and there we have water!

In many places, it is necessary to boil or filter water to remove any leftover dirt and germs and make it safer to drink.

Simple ways to conserve water

We can save water at home by following a few simple tips:

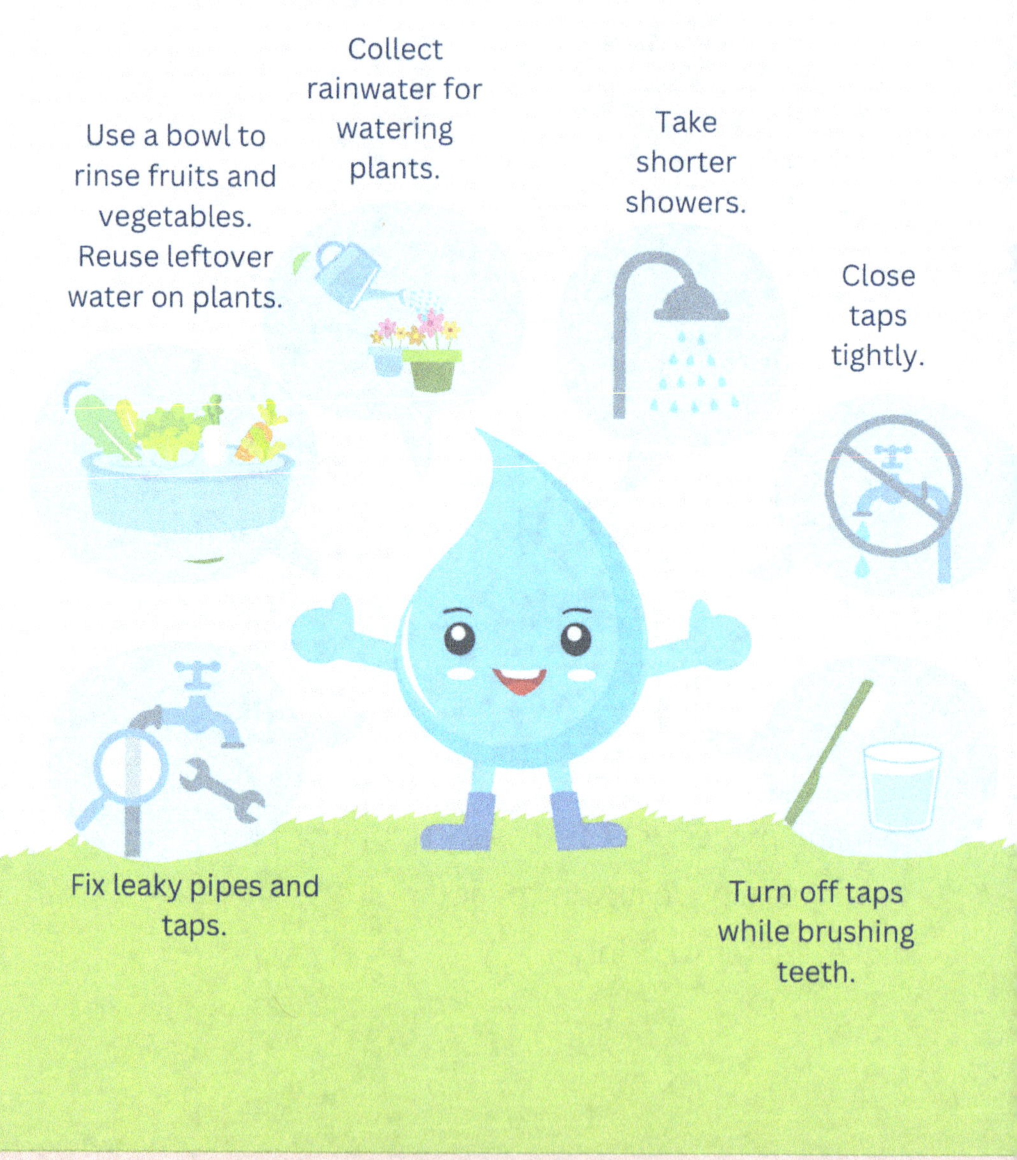

Jungle Word Search

How many animals can you see on this page?
Can you find all of them by scanning each row (left to right) and column (top to bottom) in the grid below?

I Am Thankful For...

Lea learns about gratitude from her friend Tina. Tina tells her how much fun her days are turning out to be since she started doing a gratitude list.

All she does is to think about all the nice things that made her smile that day and list them down on a paper.

Inspired by Tina, Lea goes home and tries to come up with a list of all the nice things that brought her joy too, since that morning. She could quickly recall many happy and fun things, without much effort.

Satisfied with her first gratitude list, she proudly hangs it on the kitchen refrigerator door for everyone else to see.

Though there were a few things that had bothered Lea during the day, like getting upset over a lost book or an argument with her brother, now they seemed so small when Lea recalls her day's events while making the list.

Lea had many more pleasant things to be happy about. Seeing how this little task had turned out to be fun and made her day so delightful, she decides to continue making the gratitude list every day to count her small and big blessings.

What is gratitude?

Gratitude is to be thankful for the good things we have. We can only be thankful for the things that we notice.

What can I be grateful for?

All of us can be thankful for so many things we come across every day.

We are surrounded by our family and friends who love and care for us. We can be grateful for our clothes, food, toys and books. We can appreciate so many amazing things in nature like trees, animals, sun, rain, flowers and so on.

Why do we have to be grateful?

Gratitude is a positive emotion that helps us to feel good, in turn helping our body and mind to function better.

When we start to appreciate what we have, it makes us feel blessed and keeps our mood up to focus better on our daily tasks.

When we are happy, we also get along well with our family and friends.

What do we do about the things that we are not grateful for?

There are days when things do not go as we expect, maybe at school, with friends or at home.

Though these things can upset us, we can still look for any good thing to be thankful for in those situations or just be thankful for what we can learn from those things.

For example, when we walk on a slippery or wet floor, if we are not careful enough we can slip and get hurt. In such a situation, we can be thankful for having learned to be more careful while walking on wet areas and avoiding future accidents.

How do we express gratitude?

We are free to choose what we think about anything. So we can make it a habit to think positively and appreciate all the kind people and nice things we come across every day, be it small or big.

There are many ways to express our gratitude. We can do whichever way works best for us.

Saying "Thank You" out loud to appreciate someone who helped us out.

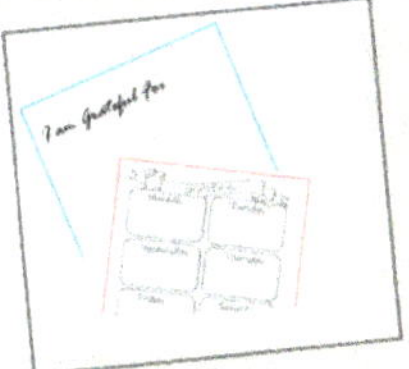

Writing about what we are thankful for in a notebook, paper, or gratitude diary.

Drawing or painting what we appreciate.

Thinking about favourite parts of the day before sleeping.

Try it yourself!

Below is a simple gratitude list that you can use.

Try out the gratitude exercise for a week. Every day, note down two to three things that made you happy, that were fun or made you feel better.

SUNDAY

MONDAY

TUESDAY

WEDNESDAY

THURSDAY

FRIDAY

SATURDAY

I Can Do It

You could see no one else as close as Maya and Roy. They were like peas in a pod. The two friends held each other dearly.

Maya and Roy were always alike, except for one thing. They handled their challenges differently.

It was a sunny afternoon in the park. Maya and Roy were by the pond, among the reeds and grass. They were trying to skip stones in the water. Maya's father recently taught them how, and they were trying to do it on their own.

Roy was getting more frustrated by the second. Since they started, he had not skipped a single stone.

"Ugh! This is silly!" Roy pouted.

"It's okay," Maya comforted. "Let's try again. I bet we can get it next time."

She had not skipped a single stone, either.

"You said that seven 'next times' ago," whined Roy with a stomp.

"It is still a 'next time', though. You just got to believe."

Roy sat down and placed his chin on his hands. "But what if we never get it?"

Maya threw another stone. It just sank into the water.

"Then we have to try harder. My dad said that believing in yourself wins half the fight."

Roy threw another stone, and it still sank.

"So we should be 50 percent winning by now. Why does it feel like 100 percent losing?"

"That is why," Maya pointed out. "How can you believe in yourself when you think that you're a loser?"

Roy thought hard on what Maya said. "Why haven't you skipped stones if you believe in yourself that much?" He tested.

"'Cause I believe we do everything together so I'll only be able to skip stones when you could."

The two friends laughed.

"You're silly, Maya."

"The same goes for you".

Roy realized that he has to believe in himself. That is because he can do many things when he believes in himself. Besides, Maya believes in him.

"We will do our best, when we think we can do it!" Maya assured him.

Roy took a deep breath and picked up a smooth stone from the ground, which looked perfect for skipping.

With a new determination, he held the stone with a firm grip, as taught by Maya's father. He raised his hand and threw the stone.

Skip! Skip! Plop! The stone bounced off twice this time before sinking in the water.

"Hooray!" the two friends cheered. Maya threw her stone, and it skipped as well.

"The two friends continued to skip stones and cheer for each other as the day went by.

Soon, the sun was beginning to set, and it was time to go home.

It was a long walk to their houses. Maya and Roy had never gone home this late before.

"What if we got lost?" Maya started to tremble with fear.

"Don't worry. I am here. I know the way like the back of my hand. We will reach home before it is dark." Roy assured.

"How can you be so sure?" Maya frowned.

"What happened to all that talk we had earlier? We have to believe in ourselves that we can do this, remember?"

"Well, It's easy to believe in simple things like skipping stones."

"You know what?" Roy teased. "All big things start with small steps. Come and hold my hand.
Let us take little steps and reach home slowly."

Maya smiled and held onto Roy's hand tightly.

The two children walked together, holding hands and looking around keenly. Further and further they walked, Maya's heart filled with pride. She was so proud of her friend Roy. He did truly believe in himself.

"Self-belief is the key, I think." She blinked.

"What did you say?" Roy asked, as he continued to lead the way.

"Nothing," Maya laughed.

Roy shook his head, though Maya could not see it.

"Well, I bet you'll say something now. Look right up ahead."

"We're home! Great job, Roy!"

"Well, I wouldn't have done it if you weren't there. I would not have learned to believe in myself."

"Speaking of believing, why don't we skip more stones tomorrow?" Maya invited.

"Sure! Tomorrow, you'll see! I will skip a boulder!"

Spot the Difference !

Can you find 10 differences between the 2 pictures?

Can you spot a mouse?

Festivals Around the World

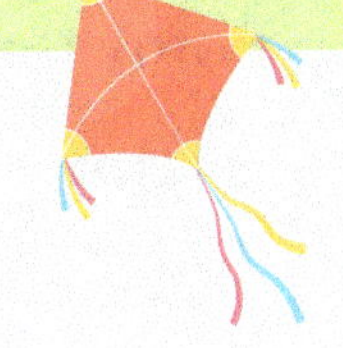

Festivals are full of fun and excitement.

They are joyous occasions that we look forward to every year to celebrate with our loved ones.

Each festival is special and is celebrated at a specific time of the year and has its own significance.

There are so many festivals celebrated around the world for different reasons.

Some festivals celebrate special or important events related to the place we live. Some are related to the religion people follow, while some are to celebrate the changing seasons.

Let's see some of the popular festivals around the globe.

Brazilian Carnival takes place for three to four days in different cities in Brazil. The carnival is known for its colourful costumes, music, singing, and dancing.

Thousands of people gather to see the large parades with decorated floats and people dressed in bright costumes and fancy masks.

Cherry Blossom Festival is a popular spring celebration in Japan. People gather for picnics and parties under the cherry trees.

The trees are in full bloom over a two-week period in spring.

Lanterns are hung on the trees and are lit up at night to enjoy the viewing of beautiful cherry blossoms.

Christmas is an important festival for Christians across the world to celebrate the birth of Jesus. Christmas cards are sent to friends and family members to express good wishes.

Celebrations involve singing carols, decorating a Christmas tree with lights and ornaments, exchanging gifts, and enjoying special meals with friends and family members.

Day of the Dead Festival is celebrated in Mexico and in many parts of Latin America to remember the loved ones who have died.

People decorate altars at home and the graves with flowers, candlelight, favourite food, and things of their loved ones who have passed away.

Celebrations also include decorations and sweets in the shape of skulls and skeletons.

Diwali is the festival of lights celebrated by Hindus, Sikhs, and Jains, in India, Nepal, and around the world. People decorate their homes with a lot of lights to celebrate the victory of light over darkness.

Bright and colourful patterns called rangoli are drawn on the floors of the house.

Friends and families gather to celebrate with special sweets, festival meals and bursting firecrackers.

Hanukkah is a festival of light, celebrated by Jews for eight days. Menorah, a special candle holder with multiple arms, is lit during this festival.

They start with one candle and add a new candle on each of the eight nights.

Family and friends gather for festive meals and exchange gifts. Children play a fun game called "dreidel" using a four-sided spinning top.

Moon Festival, also known as the Mid-Autumn festival, is celebrated in many countries of Asia to worship the moon and give thanks for the harvest. Friends and families gather outdoors to enjoy the moonlight.

They make flying lanterns, which are lit up and sent soaring into the night sky.

Mooncake, in the shape of a full moon, is a traditional food that people enjoy eating during this festival.

Ramadan is a special month for Muslims around the world. During Ramadan, many elders observe fasting. That means, they do not eat or drink after the sunrise until the sunset.

At the end of Ramadan, "Eid al-Fitr" is celebrated, where special prayers are held in mosques and families and friends get together for a grand feast and exchange gifts.

Thanksgiving Day is celebrated in the U.S, Canada and many places around the world to give thanks for all the food the harvest has brought and other blessings of the past year.

Families come together to celebrate with a special feast that usually includes turkey, mashed potatoes and pumpkin pie. Some people practise gratitude by volunteering at charities or by helping people in need.

Do you know what is common across different festivals celebrated around the world?

Sharing love and kindness with our loved ones and gratitude for the things we have through the celebration, that include delicious food, gifts, decorations, and lots of fun activities.

Trivia

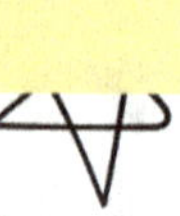

1. Which is the largest animal that has ever lived on Earth?

2. What is another name for maize?

3. Which is the world's largest ocean?

4. What is a year with 366 days called?

5. Which is the closest star to the Earth?

6. Are there more black keys or white keys on a piano?

7. What is the smallest country in the world?

8. What is the largest organ in the human body?

9. Which bird can fly backwards?

10. Which sport is also known as "ping-pong"?

Answers on page 115

Origami Pen Holder

What you'll need :

- 6 colourful papers, each of size 21 x 21 cm
- 6 strips of colourful or patterned paper, each of size 10 x 5.2 cm
- Scissors
- Craft glue
- Ruler
- Cardboard of size at least 12 x 12 cm
- Coloured paper to cover both the sides of the cardboard

What to do:

Step 1: Take one 21 x 21 cm paper and follow the folding method shown below. Do not forget to crease after every fold for all the steps below.

1. Fold the paper into half on one side. Then unfold the paper.

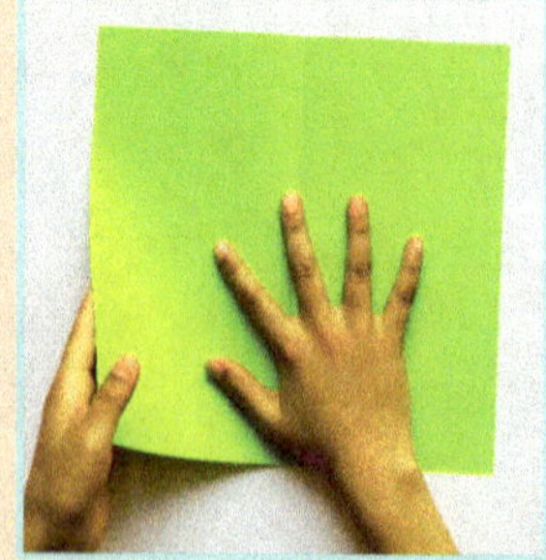

2. Fold the paper into quarters on both sides.
   Then unfold the paper.

3. Repeat Steps 1 and 2 for the other edge of the
   paper. Then fold the four corners into triangles.

4. Fold the paper with triangular corners in half.
   Then reverse the side.

5. Fold again to bring both the sides to the centre. Then insert a 10 x 5.2 cm strip into the triangle opening and lock the sides into each other.

6. Adjust on both the sides until the strip is in the center to get one block ready. Repeat the above folding method of Step 1 with five more (21 x 21 cm) coloured papers. Now you have all the six block ready.

Step 2: Take any two blocks. Apply glue on one side of a block and stick this to a side of another block. Make sure the strips are visible on both the blocks.

Step 3: Take the cardboard piece. Place the hexagonal block over it and mark the outline. Cut the cardboard over the outline drawn.

Step 4: Place the cut cardboard over a coloured piece paper and draw the outline of the hexagonal block, leaving an additional space of at least 1 cm. Cut the paper along the outline. Cut the cardboard over the outline drawn.

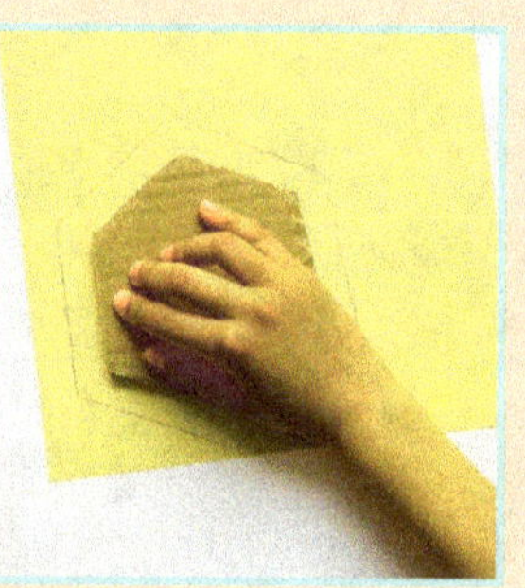

Step 5: Place the cut cardboard piece over the centre of the cut paper and fold the paper inwards along the edges of the cardboard. Trim the extra paper strips and apply glue on one side of the coloured paper. Place the cardboard over it and stick the paper on all sides.

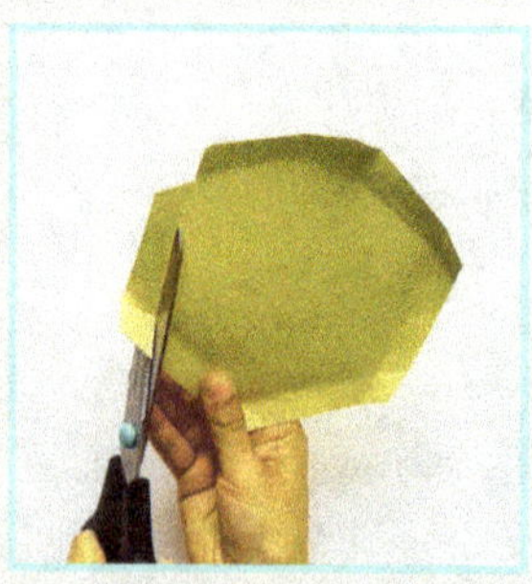

Step 6: Place the cardboard again on the leftover coloured paper and draw an outline. Cut it along the outline. Apply glue on the open side of the cardboard and stick the cut coloured paper over it. Now the base of the pen holder is ready.

Step 7: Apply glue on all the edges of the bottom side of the hexagonal block and stick the cardboard base. Allow the glue to dry.

The hexagonal pen holder is ready!

Keep your pens, pencils, and other stationery items in this creative and colourful origami pen holder.

How Do I Handle Teasing?

What if someone makes fun of me or says or does something mean? How do I respond?

It is okay to feel upset, as it can hurt my feelings. I cannot control what others say or do. *But, I can choose how I respond!*

I can choose not to react and walk away from the person when possible.

I can spend time with someone who is nicer to me or play with something I like.

I can respond by telling them how I was hurt by what they said or did.

I can ask for help from an adult around, someone I trust.

Let us not make fun of others, as teasing hurts the other person as much as it does to us when someone is teasing us. Let us always be kinder to ourselves and others!

The Little Prince

Once, a young pilot while flying his plane, crash landed in the Sahara Desert.

As he was busy fixing the plane, a little boy came to him and asked him to draw a little lamb.

A little perplexed, the pilot recalled the only drawing he had ever made when he was a child.

He remembered drawing a boa constrictor, a large snake which had a huge belly from eating a whole elephant. All the grownups he had showed it to said it looked like a hat. A little disappointed that no one understood him, he had stopped drawing.

Heeding the little boy's wish, the pilot took out a pen and paper out of his pocket and drew a little lamb. But it didn't look like a lamb at all for the boy.

The pilot made a few more attempts to draw the lamb. But the boy turned them all down.

The frustrated pilot, wanting to get back to his repair work, just drew a box with three holes. He told the boy that the lamb was inside the box.

To the pilot's amazement, the face of the little boy lit up. It was exactly what the boy was looking for.

The pilot came to know the boy as "the little prince", who revealed his story bit by bit.

He had golden hair and a lovable laugh. He kept repeating his questions until they were answered.

The little prince came from a tiny asteroid far away from the Earth. The asteroid was almost the size of a house. It had nothing but three volcanoes, some baobab plants and a beautiful rose plant.

The little prince spent his days looking after his tiny planet. He kept his planet safe by cleaning the volcanoes and plucking out undesirable baobab plants.

He wanted a lamb to eat away those unwanted plants.

The little prince adored the rose and took great care of it. He admired her beauty and her fragrance. To protect the delicate rose from wind and caterpillars, he even made a glass dome.

Over time, the rose became increasingly difficult to please. Though he loved the rose, the little prince grew tired of her unending demands and decided to leave the asteroid.

With a heavy heart, bidding farewell to the rose, the little prince set off on his journey to explore the universe.

He wandered through space and visited six different planets before reaching the earth.

Each planet had only one strange grown-up.

On the first planet, the little prince came across a king who loved ordering. But he issued only such orders that could be obeyed, such as ordering the sun to set!

The second planet was inhabited by a person who considered himself to be the most admirable person. But he was the only person on his planet!

On the third planet lived a person who drank all the time to forget his drinking problem!

The fourth planet had a businessman who was always busy counting the stars he owned. He had no time to look at the real beauty of the stars!

The fifth planet was so small that a full day was over in a minute! The lamplighter who lived there had to light the lamppost every few seconds to mark the night.

On the last planet, he met a geographer who recorded special things like oceans, mountains, and deserts across the universe, without actually visiting any of them. The geographer told the little prince about the uniqueness of flowers and advised him to visit the Earth to see more flowers.

Confused by the grownups and their strange obsessions, the little prince arrived on Earth, landing in the Sahara Desert.

He was greeted by a mysterious yellow snake. The snake claimed to have a special power and offered to help the little prince return home, if he ever wished.

On his continued journey on Earth, the little prince encountered many curious things. And among them was a garden full of roses. After seeing so many roses that looked like his rose, he felt sad.

His own rose was not as unique as he had imagined. He laid down on the grass and cried and cried until a friendly fox came along.

The fox wished to be tamed by the little prince. He explained that taming would create a special bond of love and connection between them. The little prince spent a lot of time with the fox, taming him and grew close to him gradually.

But soon came the time for the little prince to leave the fox to continue his travels.

Before saying his goodbyes, the tearful fox revealed to the little prince a great secret.

"The most important things can only be seen with the heart, and not with the eyes".

The little prince realized from the fox that his rose was indeed very special for him.

He had tamed the rose over time. He had lovingly taken care of her by watering, by cleaning, and by protecting her. His rose was more precious to him than all the other beautiful roses he had seen on Earth.

The little prince longed to go back to his planet to see his rose.

He remembered his old friend, the yellow snake, he had met in the desert and decided to take his help to return home.

On his way to the snake is when the little prince befriended the pilot and asked him to draw a lamb.

The little prince was also worried that the lamb could eat his special rose. So, the pilot drew a muzzle for the little lamb and handed him the drawing.

Parting from the pilot, the little prince told him to look at the stars whenever he remembered him.

The pilot who finally managed to repair his plane left the desert, with fond memories of the little prince, his wonderful stories, and his unwavering loyalty to his rose.

Story Time Quiz

- What did Pip learn to love about himself, after accompanying the clown around the city?

- Is there some thing that's unique about you, that you would like to embrace just as Pip did?

- What secret did the fox reveal to the little prince?

- What helped Roy succeed in skipping stones?

- Is there any skill you are currently working on, that you want to get better at?

- What did the king realise about the most important time, the most person and the most important thing to do?

- Why didn't Jay say anything to his mom when she noticed the missing flowers? Could he have handled the situation differently?

Some days it is hot, and some other days it is cold. It rains continuously sometimes and other times it is snowing, windy or dry. Sometimes, leaves fall off trees and at another, trees leaf out and bloom.

That is because nature goes through a cycle of changes every year, called *seasons*.

We know that our planet Earth is revolving around the sun and is also rotating around its axis at the same time.

This axis is an imaginary line that connects the north and south poles on the Earth. The axis is slightly tilted, affecting the amount of sunlight each place on the Earth gets every day, causing the seasons to change.

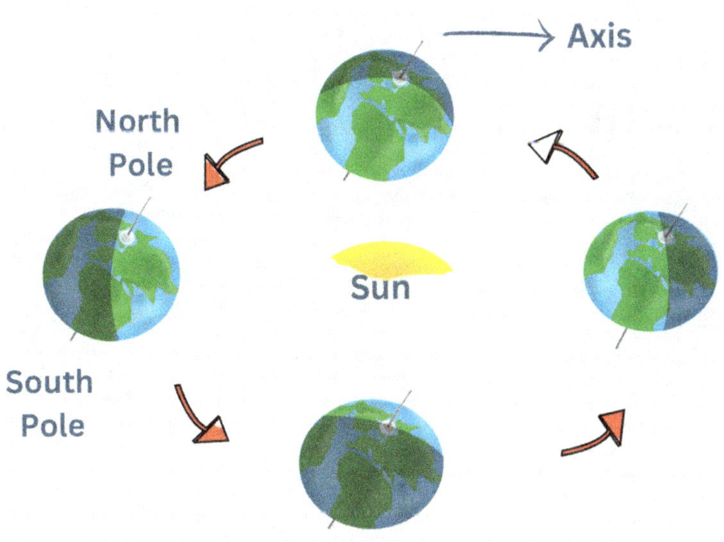

The changing seasons influence what we eat, what we wear, how we commute, festivals we celebrate, and so on.

Plants and animals are also affected enormously by seasons. Each season plays an important role, helping them in their cycle of growth and changes.

Seasons are not the same in all places on the Earth.

In many parts of the world, there are four seasons. They are spring, summer, autumn and winter.

Let's take a look at what is special in each of these seasons.

Spring season marks the end of cold winter days and the beginning of warm and sunny days.

Spring is the season of new beginnings with more greenery emerging as plants and trees grow new leaves and flowers start to bloom.

Animals become more active. Hibernating animals wake up from their long sleep and migratory birds arrive from their winter homes.

Spring festivals are celebrated in many places to welcome the new season.

Summer is the hottest season of the year with longer days and shorter nights.

In many countries, schools are closed for summer break, giving time to go on long vacations or spending more time with family and friends.

It is also the time to relish cooling watermelons and ice creams or head towards beaches or pools to cool off and have fun swimming.

Nature is in full bloom with bright-coloured flowers and beautiful butterflies hovering over the nectar-rich flowers.

It is essential to stay hydrated by drinking a lot of water or fruit juice and also to wear light coloured cotton clothes.

Autumn is the season of transition from summer to winter, when the days start to get shorter and cooler.

This season is also called "Fall" since leaves fall off of specific trees (called deciduous trees) like maple or oak. Leaves on such trees start to change colour from green to red, orange, yellow or brown before falling.

Animals begin to prepare for winter by growing thick fur, stocking up food or migrating towards warmer places to avoid food scarcity and cold weather.

It is the season to explore corn mazes at farms or enjoy pumpkin soups or pies at home.

Winter is the coldest season of the year with chilly mornings, shorter days, and longer nights.

It snows in many places, allowing people to enjoy winter sports like skiing, sledding, or ice skating.

Some trees look bare with no leaves. Some animals like bears, bats, frogs and snakes living in their natural habitat go into a long sleep, as it is harder for them to find food.

We wear warm clothes to keep out the cold and consume warm food and drinks to warm us up.

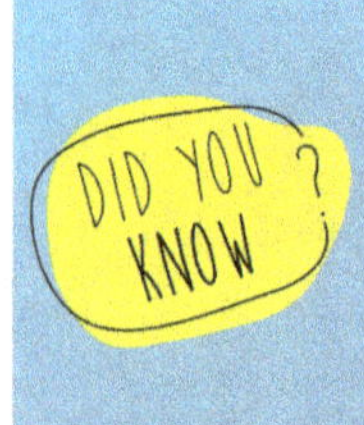

Seasons happen at different times in different parts of the world. When it is summer in the northern part of the Earth (the US or Europe), it is winter in the southern part (Australia or South America).

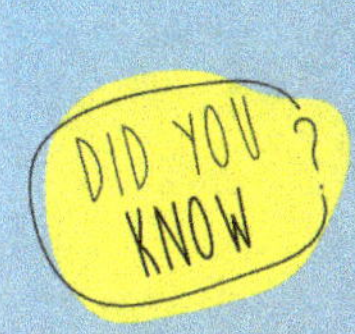

We go through different seasons over the year.

Each season is important as it brings with it the required changes in the climate, allowing plants and animals to flourish.

With something to look forward to, each season is unique for all of us.

How Well Do I Know Myself?

1. If have to name one thing I am really good at, it's ....

2. My least favorite game is .... because ....

3. An activity that I enjoy so much when time just flies: ....

4. When I am feeling down or sad, I like to .... that cheers me up.

5. I love the smell of .... and the sound of   ....

6. Something nice I say to myself is ....

Fruit and Nut Smoothie

Fruits and nuts are super healthy snacks. They are loaded with different nutrients that help us stay strong, fit and healthy.

If you are feeling tired or weak and need some quick energy during a busy day, drink a glass of water and grab some fruit or nuts to eat.

If you are in the mood for a little adventure and fun in the kitchen, try making this fruit and nut smoothie. It is easy to make and delicious to taste.

What you will need:

For a glass of smoothie

- 1 ripe banana
- 1/2 cup (125 ml) of chilled milk
- 1/4th cup (50 g) of a mix of dry fruits and nuts (for example: 4 dates, 5 cashews, 5 almonds, 10 raisins and 3 walnuts)

What you have to do:

1. Soak the dry fruits and nuts in warm water for 30 mins.

2. After 30 mins, strain and rinse the dry fruits and nuts. Discard the water.

3. Slice the banana into smaller chunks carefully.

Ask for the help from an adult for using the blender for the following step.

4. Place banana, dry fruits and nuts in a blender. Blend them into a smooth paste. Then, add the milk and give it a quick blend for a few seconds .

Pour the smoothie into a glass and enjoy!

If you would like a different flavoured smoothie the next time, instead of banana, use fruits like apple, mango or berries (use 3/4th of a cup or around 110g of fresh fruit chunks). You can vary the quantity and the type of dry fruits and nuts as you like.

Pawsome Friends!

Find the 10 differences!

Riddles

1. Your name
2. A clock
3. A towel
4. Silence
5. A battery
6. Two
7. Seven
8. Every month
9. A plate
10. Darkness

Can you spot a mouse?

Trivia

1. The blue whale
2. Corn
3. The Pacific Ocean
4. A leap year
5. The Sun
6. White keys
7. Vatican City
8. The skin
9. The hummingbird
10. Table tennis

Jungle Word Search

Inspiring a ♥

of Reading and Learning

Did you enjoy the book?

We love hearing your feedback and
ideas for the upcoming series.
Write to us @
www.rainbow-kids.app/feedback.